Chasing the Hoopoe

Chasing the Hoopoe

John Weston

First published in 2005
by Peterloo Poets
The Old Chapel, Sand Lane, Calstock,
Cornwall PL18 9QX, U.K.

A catalogue record for this book is available
from the British Library

ISBN   1-904324-28-2

Printed in Great Britain by
Antony Rowe Ltd, Chippenham, Wilts.

ACKNOWLEDGEMENTS

Acknowledgements to the following, where some of these poems, or versions of them, first appeared: *The Guardian, The Spectator, The Independent on Sunday,* the BBC *Today* Programme, *Critical Survey, The London Magazine, The Rialto, Agenda, Magma, The Interpreter's House, The Shop, Poetry Scotland, Envoi, Poetry Life, Scintilla, Other Poetry.*

The poem *A Galapagos Sequence* recaptures a visit in 1997: my guide books included: *Satan Came To Eden* by Dore Strauch (Harper 1936); *Floreana* by Margret Wittmer (Michael Joseph London 1961); *The Enchanted Islands* by John Hickman (Nelson 1985); and *Beak of the Finch* by Jonathan Weiner (Knopf 1994).

Thanks for their encouragement to Mimi Khalvati, to Jane Duran, and especially to my wife Sally.

To the Memory of my Mother and Father

'If the risk you took
is now your element, be free in it, begin
the braving of new surfaces . . .'
John Mole
(*The Waterfall*)

CONTENTS

I. At Home

II. Out of Doors

III. City

IV. Cycle of Cathay

I. At Home

The Launch

(For Marcus Cumberlege)

I do not remember the house
where I was born, though the poem
(in my mother's voice) opened on
more than the sun's little window.

I must have grown ears like errant
wings at school when they recited
spells for how to gyre and gimble,
spread butter with the carpenter.

I tasted mellow fruitfulness;
saw silent flock in woolly fold;
wondered about his last duchess,
golden lamps, vegetable love,

and whether fifty springs sufficed
to stop winter icummen in.
I listened to Greek frogs croaking,
the ripple of Sabine fountain.

But you followed jumblies to sea
with 'sails as frail as autumn leaves',
leaving me standing in the lea
with 'less than one good line a day'.

It makes me think of my first bike –
the Coventry, and how they had
to push and push to get me to
take off; and the birdlike grace of

equilibrium finally
achieved, the blessing of surprise
at discovering that no hands
could mean flying even faster.

My Father

He emerges from
the pages of his never-
to-be published verse
gesturing to me, as with
some forgotten semaphore –

'The Shrapnel Gleaners',
'Oak Trees', 'Afternoon Alert'.
So I too glean shards
from blitzed childhood memories,
rebuild his fractured presence,

matching his phrases
to precarious glimpses
over a lifetime,
and seeking now to summon
his ghost out of the shadows

for a belated
Festschrift. What coded sequence
has pushed my pen to
themes or images later
found prefigured in his own?

Broken health, broken
love – these poems I value
more now: lineaments
of a disappointed life,
but an honest monument.

It speaks still, the voice
comes and goes, as I read them,
eclipsing absence;
his own words like a handshake:
'How I pray he will not grieve'.

War Games

(To an early friend)

Your hop-hop seemed okay to me: the leg braced,
lame boot mounted as if on half a bedpost,
fit to face anything they said could rain down
after the siren.

As you launched each perfectly balanced paper
aeroplane (flattened delta wings, a bookmark
tail) from your right hand short of half its fingers
which was a makeshift

V for victory or a kind of inbuilt
bone catapult to scarify the rivals
poaching our sticklebacks and young tomatoes
from the allotments,

you, Colin, spelled for me the Wartime Hero.
Trim to a fault, despite the left fist playing
less than its own full house, your models rolled out
covered with decals –

Spitfires, Hurricanes, Blenheims by the squadron,
like some swarm from a sorcerer's apprentice:
I could only marvel at such bravura
multiplication.

Then came early betrayal: Enfield targets
drew the sniping doodle-bugs; once I saw them
cut off by high aces, the lazy smoke plumes
signing the blue air,

balsa and airfix magic blew to pieces.
At that moment I wakened to a keener
itch for the shrapnel jag, the blaze of windows
shattering daily;

thought I caught a different accent on the
wireless after the pips, and other turnings
beckoning to me as I learned to fly my
Coventry Eagle.

Dead ends mostly, and still no All Clear's sounded
down the years, as we watch the nightly maimings.
Peace to you, model maker (hoping you'll hop
out of a phone book)!

Talisman

This Victorian penny,
bullet hole punched at the rim
where it winged the old Queen's crown,
has sat on my key-ring since

I filched it from The White Hart's
till, half a century back,
for luck. FID DEF's never let
me down, though the coin has worn

communion-wafer thin,
and in just one hundred years
the embossed flag has faded
from the shield of Britannia,

whose head (or what was left by
the wound exiting the oth-
-er side) is now floating in
a feuillemorte Valhalla cloud.

If I tilt it to the light,
the royal gaze is fixed, but
the lips move, the cheek allows
a faint porphyry blush. Touch,

it's my aged aunt's soft kiss
when she came in from the snow.
I pinch it between finger
and thumb, chafe the used metal.

Out of the Blue

email bermuda: *'Are you by chance the JW*
for whose teddy-bear I once traded my camera ,
at Elcot, near Kintbury, it must have been '48?
I still have the bear (called 'JW' from that date).
If I'm right, whatever became of the little box camera?
If mistaken, I really am sorry to trouble you.'

Soon a careful hand-written letter arrives,
the teddy-bear's photo enclosed. My God, I remember!
My Mother had given me him just after the War.
Still un-demobbed in khaki and scarlet, the bear
fixes me sternly, his eyes flashing jet and amber,
arms stretched in resignation. No Kodak survives.

'Elcot' – the shape of this word releases a flood:
childhood paradise of coppice and garden acres,
tall Wellingtonias with the spongy bark,
cock pheasants at ease among the boxed hedge-work,
nectarines fattening on the walled espaliers,
an abandoned orchard, a piggery beyond the wood

for hunting rats with an airgun, tame ferrets
in the converted hen-coop, my hidden 'residence'
up the copperbeech where I counted my secret hoard.
Hotel & Country Club said the painted board
after period fashion. The permanent residents
took tea from a silver urn. County friends would collect

later for cocktails and dinner ('Do try the jugged hare')
under a portrait rumoured to be by Gainsborough.
The radiogram 78s were Victor Silvester
and Edmundo Ros. Snooker or a round of canasta
crowned the extended evening. When finally through,
'Nothing else like it for miles around' they'd declare.

It went bust of course. On the day for counting debts
my mother took off in her '39 Sunbeam, threatening
to kill herself. Hot in the wake to retrieve her
on Matchless 500 roared the official receiver
who stopped her in time. That same winter evening
I wept to be told we must go, leaving even the dogs.

The teddy-bear I suppose I must have outgrown,
or found was ill-matched to a boarding school address,
or perhaps never liked that much. The Brownie swap
(I'd thrown in an acrobat too) now sounds quite a snip:
is there more than a hint she gave it up under duress,
not quite trusting the words about parents' permission?

If so, no amount of diplomatic banter
can make amends to her now. Still, we're as one:
those random exchanges proved to hold a value
beyond the bargain under a Berkshire apple-tree,
like a child's balloon that has wafted across the ocean
and summons the past, and makes the world seem smaller.

The Slip

Do you recall that day on the clinker, when
pitching from Carrigillihy over to
    Seal Island stretched out on the skyline,
  suddenly we saw the waves get higher?

How can we joke at what we were risking, with
children so small and no-one to notice our
    plight from up on the gorsy headland,
  Sullivan's boat shipping slaps of water?

Near misses, each remembers a later one:
car hurtling backwards (a burst) on the motorway;
    knife at the throat in Spain; the last gasp
  life-saving help from a Transkei rip-tide,

medal awarded. What do you make of it?
Should we insure all risks, should we hire a good
    lawyer, or contact Health & Safety,
  hoping there might be a claim to trade on?

Danger can teach how to trust. Fragility
rules. I could fall tomorrow. Today I still
    bless return to a sloping jetty,
  our summer days at 'The Slip' to launch them.

Last Rites

That final day in Bedford hospital
the car-park man ticked me off, as I came out
'You can't leave yours there, you know.' 'I do know,'
I answered 'but your mother only dies once.'

She'd never adjusted to a life without work –
her bank of interests had too little left to draw on.
So in the small hours, when breathless anxiety struck,
comfort was slight, and I knew I was out of my depth.

'None of that sort of thing in *our* family' she insisted
when I rescued her from a psychiatric ward.
She was convinced they were secretly plotting against her,
which would have been funny except for her haunted eyes.

The end near, I was called to a different bedside.
She seemed more puzzled than frightened, even slightly
                                        indignant
when I ventured on her a passage from *Revelation*,
as if to say 'Not much of *that* in the family either.'

Her insistent 'Goodbye' at my whispered goodnight
before snatching sleep in an adjacent room
I realised only afterwards had meant what it said,
for with the dawn she sighed deeply, and stopped.

Her face suffused with a Lenten purple blush.
Kneeling I kissed her, drew the rings from her finger,
then rose to leave the orderlies to their business.
I felt she'd launched on *Gerontius'* great journey,

me on the nearer shore applauding her brave
life and her exit from it. In Ampthill churchyard,
'See, they return, and bring us with them' the stone said.
When at last I went back to clear her belongings,

as if possessed by a sudden mythic force
I fell on her bed, and felt bodying forth
a primal surge, an upwelling torrent of grief,
sucking the breath out of me – a raw howl

the ear could hardly recognise as my own.
Knocking at the door, a neighbour below enquired
politely if a cup of tea might help, her gesture
the cue for all the familiars to reassemble.

House at Denbigh Gardens

Bricks-and-mortar craft
buoyant in gravel eddies,
continental drift,
tacks for a new century,
hull down in the solar wind.

Inside, solid as
an Edwardian liner
and dressed overall,
it welcomes each boarding pair
with whisper of timber torque.

Anchored asylum
from 'earth filled with violence',
its constant bearing
has helped 'keep the seed alive',
hallow space for survival.

It survived bomb sticks
last time. The coloured glass panes
we restored to type;
from the garden's tidal depths
I still dredge shelter concrete.

One day we'll cast off
old moorings, when leaves lift at
intimations of bugles
(the windows wink knowingly,
 they have seen it all before) –

we shall look westward
over Mount Ararat Road,
seek that band of cloud
sailors know as Noah's Ark,
the wake stretching behind us.

Garden Shed

'Summerhouse' I say,
because light entering holds
day-long like a lens
and the redwood walls exhale
all year a fume of sunshine.

From within mark how
hollyhocks and lupins crowd
the magnolia
to watch spider and titmouse
invest their precious seconds.

Put oil to the scarred
workbench, spin the vice-jaws tight,
polish the copper
cauldron, for fully loading
with logs of cherry and ash.

Make sure to inspect
tools on parade, bikes, mower.
Adjust tarred roof-tiles.
Let water-butt, compost-bin
complete suburban countdown.

No space capsule need
discover stranger planets.
Reaching forward I
throw up the window, launch to
fresh diggings, new horizons.

To Alaska and Back

I knew I was losing you that day at Brooks Camp
where we walked to see the salmon leap
into the bears' open mouths
(they didn't even have to reach out).
Face to face with the big one on the return,
'Please bear, please bear ...' you intoned trembling,
and fragmenting before my eyes.
In the hotel, as I rang our Manhattan doctor,
you lay curled like an ancient foetus toward the wall.
Back on the East River, depression's gravity towed you
into an alien orbit, inert moon of a lost planet.
No more you to talk to about the 'you',
a film had descended between us,
mirror fogged as I lifted the morning razor.
Each day's pattern fractured in the making.
For months I scanned for lost wavelengths,
knew only skin-touch of severed limbs.
You had gone missing in front of me,
the companion who'd lurched from our tent
to die in the snow.
From the madness of Alaska's sunlit nights
to the city whose canyons offer no forgiveness,
time slowed toward the higher entropy, where
zero is a loop from the window.

The day you first noticed again the sky was blue,
I wept to remember the Kodiak bear,
and counted the evening stars, as they re-emerged.

Above Normal

Implacable his gentle voice
down the line. My stomach tightens,
my words echo disembodied.

The wise course, expect further tests,
yes, he can recommend where next.
Your face is a Greek chorus mask.

Days, nights play in an altered key.
The Fates loom up from old pages:
sooner or later it's my lot.

The consultant gives a precise
percentage that there's a cancer:
this runner's no rank outsider.

Naked in blue hospital smock
I watch them go into the dark,
where with cracks like a staple gun

comes my turn to be invaded
and darts find their inner bulls-eye.
I dare not ask what X-rays show.

Six days to biopsy verdict.
You buoy me up with your life force;
mere man, I still cower at heart,

put off thinking tasks, fill hands by
sorting papers, polishing taps,
clean up the garden shed for spring –

banal count-down to what zero?
The comfort of cat's fur won't work,
my mind defaults to the worst case.

'You remember I told you there
is a one-in-seven chance you
have a tumour? The result's clear,

you are one   of the other six.'

Chastened, I wave shadows away.
They will return another day:
later not sooner, I still pray.

Grandparents

They hover like buddhas over our imaginings,
antique household gods who rode away on clouds
to make room for fresh devotions. Now occasional
visitants, leaning from framed sepia and damask
to enter the seasonal gathering at a happenstance, a phrase.

Down to earth in their day: the old man trying to salvage
a legacy's barren stake in Canadian uplands;
that grand dame, who mothered a tribe of seven
among them my father, making do in the blitzed city
and never revealing her answer to the infant's parroted
                                        question
('Granny, do *you* wear fully-fashioned bloomers?').

Entitled in turn, parents smiled on our
perpetuation of the name, as they moved from the effective
to the dignified in the family's constitution,
lavishing the little kindnesses, the hidden complicities;
and once in a while thrilling at their reach
over a generation, if a proud grandson should creep home
to show them a gasping trout hooked secretly
from the garden stream of a cordially disliked neighbour.

After their own translation, comes at length
the final act, when we lift to the news of our child's
approaching child already waving in the early scan,
and we must now busk the stage that filial piety requires,
until the last migration to that other Newfoundland where
grandparents have gone before us.

Taking Down The Cards

Night with her train of stars
falls on the frozen landscape of Kanski,
foundling girls at prayer in the chapel
gaze out over Barnes pond in winter.

Picasso's dove of peace
peeps from beneath clementine and cranberry
beyond grasp of the volunteer teaching
a mothers' group knitting in Dhankuta Nepal.

And here's the Reverend Dr Robert Walker again
skating on Duddingston Loch, heading straight for
the 1434 adoration of the kings
by way of bitterns and the RSPB .

Scrimshaw from distant soundings,
prayer-flags for the household gods,
almanac moonshine,
they deal me a concealed hand,
a flush. I watch for insinuation
of the *tarocchi*, the Wheel of Fortune
in flourished greetings, round robins.

Till next year, I play them as they fall,
push the game to the limit,
let it build a precarious
ziggurat of words and images,
lasting no longer than
the next breath.

Fifty Years On

(For Sal)

We still disagree about the exact moment:
whether the pews or the football terraces had it
and who spotted who first
in the smoky light of a Bristol afternoon.
Somehow we had fallen to walking together
and talking. I couldn't believe my luck at this turn
in what they'd arranged as a working weekend,
away from starched collars and straw boaters,
to see how the 'other half' lived in an urban parish,
courtesy of a fiery young priest called Mervyn .

The challenge in your glance seemed to signal,
beneath a hair-style borrowed from Dora Maar,
'Come on then, let's see what you're made of.'
Shyly exchanging addresses, I went back to school
hugging the biggest secret since the creation.
My early poems for you were in Latin couplets
because I hardly dared say it in English.
We both know now it was love at first sight
but for thirteen years I reckoned like a Ptolemy
before it dawned my orbit centred on you.

Random comings and goings replayed that journey
over Dartmoor to your sick-bed on my motorbike,
all skids and lost bearings under changing weather.
We each followed our own giddy diversions –
Nancy, Madrid, Dubrovnik; New York, and Hong Kong
where your delicate cast brought its fish to the rise:
at the end of your line to friends, that photograph
they casually played before me over the table
like a well presented mayfly – I took it away
and knew from that instant love could be a decision.

You stepped off the plane in your emerald coat,
and I saw this time it was real. Beneath two trees
in a Somerset lane you embraced me with your answer.
The day of our wedding I crossed the Avon Gorge
not even feeling Brunel under my feet
and still treading air when Bishop Mervyn pronounced
us man and wife in the same St Matthew Moorfields.
The de luxe dinner at Park's was £7.
Next morning we lifted off to China, joining
Li Po's journey of life, and 'sailing sunward'.

The Ming tower's armilla stood for our course
amid the din and garlic of the Peking air
and Red Guard madness raging like a Gobi dust-storm.
As the Embassy burned, the mob's blows only served
to temper your mettle. We lived and loved through it all
behind our moon-gate entrance in Sweet Rain Alley
or skating by floodlight on the Bei Hai
or hunting on bikes for a piece in yellow rosewood.
Leaving at last the blue-roofed Temple of Heaven,
did we imagine that echo of an unborn cry?

They came with a flurry, the children. I'd forgotten
how hard it was for you enacting the dutiful
mother and diplomat's wife; and how we had to
make our own beer, knead bread, and wait for the next
foreign post to recoup. From the surgeon's slab
to a career-on-the-rocks you never complained.
Our squalls blew themselves out, like Aprils of tears
washing an iris sky to the full prism
(no nimbus bruise on our horizons flagging
the late low troughs which nearly drowned us all).

Why did I always think of mandrake root
whenever we waved them off from another airport
or wrenched our life to a new peregrination,
kids growing taller in the surf, each parting
a small bereavement, which albums do not show
in the galloping carousel of summer holidays?
For you it was harder, the serial letting-go,
the vacant phases. Now, 'standing on their own feet'
they each return to us with handsome interest
your long investment of love from the beginning.

If life is opera, our curtain rose on Rossini –
the garrulous passion, the huge crescendi always
resolved in the major ; then it was *Intermezzo*
or *Capriccio*, music and words interlaced
to weave from their filigrees of conversation
a sure intimacy that brought us through
all that epic folderol of public life
(the Don Magnificos, the betrayals and disguises)
to follow instead the whisper of our glade-boat
parting the diamond waters of the Okavango.

The kernel of our love now, is it this
constant surprise of gradualness, growing
like quilts or needlepoint, the Thonet chair's rattan
you peg in strip by strip, the indoor winter
seed-dibbling, the simmering brew of oranges
that cools in jars to prick the air with kumquat;
and our garden beyond, taking on the seasons,
where you bend to a shifting tapestry of greens,
faithful to your own Ithaca, as each spring
our magnolia chases night with a thousand candles?

That recent summer's day off Druidston,
Skomer on the skyline, waves on fire with light,
a camera caught us walking out of the sea,
hands linked, a spring in our step, as if
just baptised by Botticelli's Venus.
That's how I feel with you, still.
                      Backlit
by a couching sun, the snapshot stages us
kicking over our shadows' lengthening reach
while the little breakers behind shuffle us on,
and love's tide keeps flooding up the beach

II. Out of Doors

Image

That dwarf lilac bush
is bouncing with long-
     tailed tits
   doing a jig for
the first day of spring

Behind the window
  my cat Boyo sits
   in a Zen hush
his jaws snapping
like elastic bands
    one paw

     clapping

Scillies in April

Running up to the Day-Mark
through spring heather
and high on the evening sea air,
I flushed the distant bird –
it launched on barred wings
sank fast within half a furlong
deep into cover.

All the way back at full stretch
I scanned my mind's grey branches
('look for the field-mark')
to earth the gaudy flash of
harlequin
with a sure connection;
my one recollection surely
too far outlandish.

Only after two days
did I catch Terry's mate on the
'Voyager of St Martin's',
to pep up his passengers, volunteering
'Have you heard, on Chapel Down
they've spotted a
hoopoe?'

O *upupa epops*! O song!
To have been on the mark all along!
Halloo small miracle, strange visitant,
shade of Aristophanes!
Last seen in April seven years ago
on a consular lawn
in Jerusalem.

A Wing and A Prayer

Shetlands have covered your bones from the Bronze Age.
Archbishops' banquets under Plantagenets
served up your offspring by the dishful
(cheaper than gamefowl for Lenten tables).

For Mrs Beeton, markets in London were
plentiful still with your fellow denizens
flocking from Scottish moorlands to be
netted with decoy and shot by punt gun.

By 1900 (see 'Grocer's Manual')
gourmets who prized your egg for the canapé
risked their taste being gulled by gull's eggs,
after the fenmen's pickings had dwindled.

Now in the Norfolk marshes, I'm told , there are
less than a thousand pairs of your progeny -
you, bird, who boast the longest list of
surviving names in the English language:

Lipwingle, teufit, cornwillen, horry wink,
tieve's nacket, lymptwigg, flapjack and peesieweep,
old maid, phillipene, hornpipe, wallop,
known from Fife to the fields of Bedfordshire.

'Lappewincke', let me name the eponymous
'crest' that you flag 'up and down' like the hoopoe,
who shared with you the medieval
title we all recognise as lapwing!

Green plover, lilac and bronze in the sunlight,
tumbling in wild acrobatics through airy
contours, may you increase this spring, to
fill all our skies with your deathless pibroch!

Giving Way

(The Athabasca Glacier has retreated 1.5 kilometers since 1850)

The mountains rose to a spotless sky
that morning as we approached.
At the pass, moonscape:
in a valley bulldozed by behemoth forces,
acres of claggy moraine and rock.

Walking up over the debris we counted markers
signalling at decade intervals the farthest reach
of the glacier's toe, its secular melt-back.
In a few hundred yards we passed
my birth, my matriculation,
the flurry of children, our retirement.

We ventured on to the ice flow,
the air grew chiller, water chuckled unseen.
Striding ahead up the frozen slope
toward the grin of crevasses
I heard your anxious voice calling me back.

I turned, to recognise I must be standing
at my own graveside, the coming ebb point
where the glacier's mute recessional
would not mark time for me.

Together again going down, we observed
how alpine fireweed and parnassia
had already begun to repossess the abandoned marl.

As we left the icefield and drove on,
the weather changed.

A Song of Praise

Neither the scarlet macaw nor the blue-crowned motmot,
nor the white-tipped reef-shark gliding under my flippers;
not the boa in his tree hole beside the Sierpé River,
nor yet, on her delicate egg cup, the violet sabre-wing
humbles me, as these marshalled Lilliputians.

For their trails mark the rainforest floor; and they climb
  up trees.
For their route measures ten cricket pitches; it is clear as a
  bike track.
Lo, they move ceaselessly through the humus, and up into
  the canopy:
their traffic goes orderly to and fro, keeping left like the
  English.
From the tree-tops they crop their crescent-shaped harvest;
their soldiers' bite can cut leather.

I am breathless with wonder at the order of their cosmos.
Their caravan flows like a munchkin river; their caravels
  inspire torrents of haiku.
Their leaf loads are a flutter of green sails: like wind-surfers
  they topple and recover balance.
They hold banners upright above their backs; and steer by
  the pheromones.
Kubla Khan's horsemen boasted fewer flags: Agamemnon's
  phalanx, fewer shields.
Should I drag a London bus by my teeth? My strength and
  my pride are brought low.

Red spoil lies in tons over their vaulted nests: the chambers
  of their colonies are legion.
Let me follow their tunnels deep to the roots; their
  entrances go down to the citadel.
Let me bow to their Queen, the winged victory: in the lek,
she subdues seven males; her offspring are myriad.

Let me number their dark farms in fathoms; and their
    workers in millions.
For compost they lay down their loads, to nourish their
    sacred fungus:
they husband the bloom of its milky filaments; they wait
    on mycelium.
For this is their manna, the bread that the Lord has given
    them:
this is their cult; and their manner of cultivation.

Rouse them not to wrath. Their diggings hobble the
cattle;
with their catacombs they sap foundations of buildings.
In life they take double tithe from each year's forest
    growth:
in death they bequeath their jaws as sutures for open
    wounds.
O let us not in our foolishness turn away from such lore:
let the butterfly not dazzle us with his electric blue.
For they and their scattered tribes already outnumber
    mankind;
and leaf-cutter ants shall inherit the earth.

Snow Buntings at Floyd Bennett Field

Brooklyn's old, ocean-edge runway
is lit with toadflax,

the horizon's bare of kettlepond, fence-reeds,

quahog, horseshoe-crab
do not reach,

no hawk marks
semiquavers in the air,

no bush
harbours the confusing fall warbler.

Dead low of the faded year.

They are like
memories scattering but when

those white scraps
blow skittering across forgotten tracts

I zoom all eye, clear
them quick for take-off ,

with their named blessing
return to Manhattan's hotspot

not fretting.

A Galapagos Sequence

I. Upwellings

To wake from antediluvian sleep,
Cyclopean eyelids would blink heavy in the grass:
saddlebacks wet with garúa mist
inch their hinged domes through the upland pasture
of Santa Cruz.

Afloat on the Humboldt swell, I browse
the pages of a rare edition, for the moment
when Europe's storm-clouds and *Zarathustra*
launched the wistful Germans out of their dreams
in the Tiergarten, toward errant landfall
on the pitch-lava boulders of Floreana.

'Nourmahal 1932' – cliff-face graffiti
fix that visit of Vincent Astor's yacht,
when he dined the Crusoe pair on board.
Sally Lightfoots, who danced clear
of his menu, still scamper fire-red
over the rocks, as if straight from the pot,
to be skewered on the night-heron's bill.

The courtliness of boobies is prelapsarian:
marking time, they lift then lower in turn
each sky-blue, webbed foot, like a priest
laying hands to bless; and proffer ritual twigs
to complete the minuet. Frigate-birds puff
their gullets into balloons of vermilion bubblegum,
ruminate the next act of aerial piracy.

When I dive with sea-lions
and greet the submarine penguin,
I am not thinking of fumaroles, or
the sea floor spreading in subduction of continents.

The antics of damselfish and the manta ray's
rippling coverlet distract me from the pulse
of hotspots in the deep mantle, the rising
and falling tide of earth's magma core.
A flightless cormorant semaphores with ragged stumps
that one must learn the hard way.

Basalt contours on the shoreline resolve into
basking heaps of marine iguana, who raise
mohican crests and spit salt. I wonder at days
reflected on a white sand scored only
by the aboriginal calligraphy of sea turtles
en route to bury their eggs. Everywhere such fecundity,
such animal indifference to man,
despite his pillage, puzzled even Darwin.

Giant prickly pears lend their noon shade
to relief of the carpenter bee.
Beyond the triffid mangroves, flamingos
suck water-boatmen from lagoon ooze.
At evening the short-eared owl takes post
on Genovesa's lava field, ready to ferret
the storm petrels' young from their holes.
Night moths alight to inflame the blossoms
of candelabra cactus. As darkness falls on the equator,
bottlenose dolphins patrol the islands,
luminous in the cool upwelling.

II. *Las Encantadas*

Topa Inka, summon your necromancer
who flies through the air – launch the king's balsas,
find the Islands of Fire, whose tuff and clinker
give no quarter. Even a Bishop's mass
on Passion Sunday 1535
conjures only a single hogshead of water
to keep Spanish caravel drifters alive.
Rivadeneira and his conquistadors,
fleeing the Andes demon Carvahal,
see their ensign sink with the green turtle.

To buck the spell, you merry-boy privateers
with birds on your hats, baptise the islands 'Charles',
'James', 'Norfolk', 'Albemarle' , whose shores Dampier
charts first in his round-the-world journals
(sealed in bamboo joints against the sea)
marking the anchorage depths, the abundant shark,
the fat, tame iguanas, the dildo tree,
the tortoise that can seat two men on its back –
'not unlike the top of an old hackney coach'
the captain says, and beckons his cook to approach.

'No voice, no howl, the sound of life is a hiss':
Melville's words aboard the whaler *Acushnet*
harpoon the 'emphatic uninhabitableness'
of the archipelago, even as Nantucket
grows rich on the distant bone, blubber and oil;
and passing ships watch how the melting tar
runs from their deck-seams and the ocean boils
when lava tides spill down the sides of Nar-
borough's crater. (And quietly with her landfall
another tide is turned by HMS Beagle).

A barrel-on-a-stump tells from Post Office Bay
how fortunes fail in guano, dyer's moss,
fish cannery, salt farms. Norwegian castaways
drink seals' blood to survive on Santa Cruz.
What dwindle to a feral hinterland
are goats, pigs and convicts – till Panama
opens an ocean passage to ambition, and
men draw new positions for the plans of war.
Now at world's end the Asian pirates number
their booty in shark's fins and sea cucumber.

III. Floreana (1929-1934)

People's elbows go out on desert islands:
like stepping too close to someone else's picnic,
when looks can kill. In the faded photographs
Dr Ritter is striking Faustian poses, for

Satan is coming to Eden. *O lente, lente*
currite noctis equi! Each time I read
their Gothic story I count fresh shoots
bursting from the acacia beams of his crazy hut

where his acolyte Dore hides her toothless grin
and prays for Nietzsche and Lao-tzu to be reconciled.
Hier ist der Robinson auf Galapagos,
enacting Schnabel's *Die Insel Felsenburg*

in some grand guignol of the Noble Savage,
with Punch & Judy characters jumping up
from bosky scrub and pawpaw trees, to live
out their pantomime of paradise regained.

Three spatchcocked homesteads claim this empty space
that covers twice the footprint of Manhattan:
The Wittmer children keep their parents sane –
till the grand *entrée* of that Austrian witch,

the Baroness Eloisa Wagner-Bosquet,
with her clutch of gigolos, the riding whip,
the revolver at her belt, who in a bothy
of corrugated iron hung with carpets

holds cod levée from silk cushioned divans
as 'Empress' of her demesne of Floreana.
Haphazard audience is furnished by
passing tycoons' yachts, like Captain Hancock's

who plays Schubert for them on his Gagliano,
and watches their performance open-mouthed.
Two summers, and the worm goes to the core,
rains fail, the sun hangs in a brass sky ...

Jumping from the boat I walk up Black Beach –
it's 1997, and keeping pace with the calendar
there she is, who has outlasted all,
the gründliche Frau Wittmer. White hair neat

as breakers, she signs her book 'With kind
regards', but will not stir the unrequited
ghosts from the past: the Baroness and her lover
despatched by guile to another world, so fast

her *Dorian Grey* lay open on the sand;
the rival a marooned and papery carcass;
and Dr Ritter, poisoned by botulin,
cursing with his dying utterance Dore

who, seated on his grave, seems unrepining
in the last photo before her departure.
Frau Wittmer's smile is knowing 'The others failed,
but I am happy – see here, my grandchildren.'

IV. Beak of the Finch

('These birds are the most singular of any in the archipelago' Darwin, October 1835)

```
He
        s  e t    o      u              t
                          t                o
                st      r    in        g
              o    n                e
          th      ing          t        o
        a          n      o    the  r,
      d            i g          t        o
E        ar  th'  s
              he          ar      t
        a          s          n          o
                    o      the  r.
                          E a  ch
                    f    in    ch
              s      a      n          g
              t      o
  h  i        m                the
 s      a    m                e
              t  u              n  e:
  "I      a    m                the
          r          u        n    e
                      of
t        r          u        th ,
    I    a    m                the
    s  e            a            l
                      of
t  i        m                e."
              The                  y
                  sing
                st  i  l                    l
                            t          o
                  o    u  r
          d        i g        i t a      l
        a        g            e,
        re t e        l                  l
  h  i s  The  o        r  y
                    of
                M        a    n.
T  i          g            e  r
              st      r    i        pe
            o      r
    D      N                A
              t        y            pe,
        a        l            l
                  f    i t
                        t          o
          r        u      n  the
    s  a    m                e
                    r          a c  e
  h  i s
                S      u        n
    b    e          g  a    n.
```

V. *Mutations*

Approaching *Daphne Major*'s cratered folds
I think of him beagling for the light,
Milton still in his pocket, stuffing finches
as though they had gone missing from the ark.
She looms from the hyaline like some mutant
barnacle – frond once a pillar of smoke,
operculum blown off – that has assumed
a couchant pose, waiting for the searchers
with mist-nets and calipers to return each year
who pit the caltrop against *magnirostris*
and scratch protean generations from her flank,
until she blows again or sounds and sinks
back to Gondwanaland's deep ocean drift.

Inklings, from trumpeters, scandaroons, pouters,
(his Kent study littered with cirripeds
solvitur ambulando kicking flintstones)
evolved faster than even he imagined
into the new world's adaptive landscape
where change takes place, not in Cambrian time
but with each seasons's drought or Niño flood,
the joust and jostle of the inch, as a volcano's
cloud – motionless on the horizon – to zoom lens
bulges bursts blooms in a fractal harvest,
and everywhere the finches scatter and flit
with his message to peak or niche, while in England
the peppered moth plays out his black-and-white rag.

The boat hauls anchor. My opposable thumb
turns from nuptial pad of a midwife toad,
flicks to the soapberry bug's proboscis quiver,
macaques off Japan washing sweet potatoes,
spots of the guppy, the Ozark spiderwort's
hybrid reach, then back to these islands' map
whose radials inseminate the mind,
like flametree seeds that rafted from the Guayas
to spring flamboyant out of ropy clefts
on Wolf's North shore, nature's minims
                                        selecting
my every bearing, every wild surmise, where
only the science and poetry do not compete
on our voyage of survival, always incomplete.

Waking Dream

He's the classic sleep-runner.
Once it was marathons, now
the long route round Richmond Park.
Surprising how easily
the daydream's world takes over.
Setting a dancer's axis
in balanced locomotion
he leans to forward footfalls
and his breathing syncopates
a new pulse as each sinew
and limb leaps to remember
the old prophetic summons.
These canters hone awareness:
he interprets the rose-ringed
parakeets' cachinnation,
traces bikers and moss snails
mapping root paths through nettle
and leafmould, catches the deer
poised aloof in disdain for
his fatuous urgency.
When the air is dry, feet lift
above the grass as in flight,
wrists flap loose, and in a trance
he skims up hills, coasts tree-tops,
the mind soars free, words ignite
sleeping imagination,
and with fresh hopes at his heels
he's running on and on en-
jambing the miles without pain,
till the last end-stop wakes him.

Stonypath

(For Ian Hamilton Finlay, after visiting his garden)

As if the Pentland Hills
held it like a bowl
whose water flutes on the breath,
and lost words, showering out of time,
have sown these wild acres
to a green Republic –

I hear no lark,
but as I skirt the steadings,
gold serifs start from pediments,
nouns crack open, verbs run in waves
through the moor-grass,
sigla bristle like bantams.

Sudden in gum-boots and jersey,
the old Faun flags no retreat
from Revolution's *arrosoir*, Apollo's gaze:
his carved tropes ambush my lazy eye,
his stones bridge opposites, he lades me
into fresh pools, his silent
jokes lock on like tin-fish.

Know them by their altars:
an allotment to Epicurus,
to Virgil the water source,
St Just at the broken tablets
of tomorrow's disorder,
carrier-deck, conning tower, black sails,
wind shadow made concrete
among the reeds and foxgloves.
I wind down to slow march
by the dandelion clock.

From long horizons
a small excerpt, this colourist's
great piece of turf picks out
his own history in filigree,
each thought condensed like dew
for the diligent and humble bee.

Leaving I turn. Well versed,
he melts already into Ovid's trees,
leafing the words where they fall.
Beside Lochan Eck the purple loosestrife
masses like Spartans.

Trouvaille

You sometimes come on one that seems to say
        all you could ever know
in a handful of words. If you could catch
its lattice shapes they'd melt away, like snow
        from human touch
or sleep's tide ebbing at the dream of day.

I found one such: it left me garlanded,
        danced round my ass's head
with music purer than the planets' song,
and lines as simple as beads on a thread
        and yet so strong
they lifted me to cloud nine single-handed.

I read the poem again: there is no book
        of learning makes it right,
but something given by a weightlessness
and visited on form that holds it light
        like dew on cobwebs,
seen through only if you choose not to look.

III. City

Homage to a Government

(September 2002. After Philip Larkin)

Next year we are to send the soldiers off
with moral fervour, and this is all right.
The place from World War One we got bogged down in
we now have fewer men to get bogged down in.
Crusades are meant for sending soldiers off:
in Palestine they seem to work all right.

It's hard to say who wanted it to happen.
As for the rule of law, nobody minds:
'To save successors from the scourge of war'
didn't mean Arabs really. And the war,
provided something awful doesn't happen,
may help to get Al Qaeda off our minds.

Next year our soldiers may invade the country
we founded once in post-War moral fervour
(and other tyrants can expect the same).
At home, with luck, things will be much the same.
But tell our children we're a lesser country
when common sense is ruled by moral fervour.

Still Life in New York

I.

White orchids in '*Le Périgord*'
delicate as petticoats
assume the elevated pose
of ballerinas,

their five blossoms and two unburst
lime-green buds
holding the empty restaurant's rapt attention
for the last distilled
moments of silence, until

Manhattan's garrulous lunch-hour unleashes
its vegetable onslaught,
and the dance resumes.

II.

The small Attic wine-jug,
red on black terracotta
mid fifth century BC,
depicts the young man leaving
for that war in which the sons of Oedipus
contended for the throne of Thebes
and he would be killed.

Already armed with spear and shield,
his tunic neatly pleated, he receives
from his mother's outstretched hands
the plumed helmet
that was to cover his fashionable curls
for the last time.

In sunlight from a Fifth Avenue window
the intent figures
move still among the motes,
perfectly describing a world's circle
to which no poetic line
is more than tangent.

Toward the Event

(After Bill Jacklin's etching, 2000)

Possibly I am becoming short-sighted,
but I tell you, when a crowd leans like that
it's because they feel the world
lurching under them. That's also why
they have decided to hold hands
in a semicircle, and to lift each foot
ceremoniously.

Light seeps up from the Great Lawn
like moon plasma. They will have to head for
some darker vanishing point, beyond
the helmeted man on horseback
and his startled tree. I have never seen
those steel-rigged topgallants at the Park's edge
so gaunt and stilted: as if they had
outreached themselves. It's a departure
that they reflect no windows.

Years back, one could already catch
a warning note – the radio would say
"the real thing, next time".
Now, under a sky like torn silk,
raw crepitation in the air scrambles
all divining. It seems something still escapes
our grasp of the bigger picture.
Look carefully through the glass, what do you make
of that tiny figure running?

Daisy Chain Reaction

(For Tom Phillips RA, after reading his summary treatise on ornament)

Patterns of word, like ornament
plundering nature's primal signs,
assert the mind's emblazonment,
stripes and hatchings, dots and lines.

Heraldic quarterings, as rare
as Tyrean purple, Iznik red,
mirror no language to compare
with grid and trellis that are read.

Scan tented hangings, Lenin's tomb,
feathers, or beetle's carapace,
mosaic pixels, weaver's loom,
the Hubble telescope in space;

Order the fractal's visual spell,
repeat the fish-scale imbrication,
let Shaker carpentry excel
Old Zimbabwe's crenellation;

Echo, accumulate, unfold
your eye's mnemonic treasury,
pie-crust to pot rim, dung to gold,
ochre to lapis lazuli:

No camouflage of tiger-skin,
art of acanthus or bamboo,
rivals poetic discipline,
as Dante showed he always knew,

And your vocabulary's full
of atoms which, when they combine
in verse, convert to molecule
the word's buckminsterfullerene.

Collage

(After the journals of Keith Vaughan)

Study in gouache: five ghostly figures
of gun-metal grey, blue and black sit frozen
in shared foreboding. Years after I bought it,
the full oil appeared at his retrospective,
beside the last manuscript page of his Journals,
4 November 1977...

He was quite alone in his twenty-seventh year.
The War threatened extinction, writing became
a non-combatant's alternative to what
remained of living. The painter's eye would fix
vanishing moments: as in the violet air
dust rose from the ploughboy's straining horses,
blowing like a white scarf down into the valley,
and the low sun filled the hollows with mist;
or when the wounded train crept in from France,
engine sighing on the buffers, and they offloaded
bone and flesh and bandages through the night,
till it lay in the morning light like a picked carcass.

That year, his brother was shot down and killed
four days from their casual parting in Trafalgar Square,
just at the point when they could have become friends –
their 12/50 Alvis stripped down on the kitchen table,
their drives to the Welsh coast, the tinned pilchards
slung under the exhaust to warm.
                        Now silence splintered
like night at the cock's crowing.

In Guildford gaol, to ward off claustrophobia
he drifted on a tide of Proust; 'Love to any
young cocky placed in this cell' read the graffiti.
For painting a wartime trench in a Surrey field

they fined him £25, plus confiscation;
propped on an easel in Court, this picture was
his first to be exhibited in public.

The months and years clicked on like lantern slides:
dubbin, fatigues and canvas; nomad's land –
Ilfracombe, Codford, Keighley, Belper, Leeds;
one moment soft hay and pink chestnut blossoms,
the next a village strafed and fourteen dead.
Interpreting for prisoners of war,
words failed him when they sang their *Stille Nacht*.
The curtains of his past and future drawn,
'perfection of the life or of the work'
was a choice denied him, he preferred to hold
that great art always offers, through a flaw,
a point of weakness where the heart can enter,
as in Bellini's *'Agony in the Garden'*.

When VE Day came and the flags were perched
like some new flock of rare or fabulous birds,
he sat and watched the sheep graze, as they'd done
for centuries past in Thrace and Galilee.
The Flying Fortresses flew over low,
unloaded. Then he knew the flags were real.

No flaw in Avignon's Palace of the Popes:
instead, he watched boys swimming in the Rhone;
a jealous Zeus to all young Ganymedes,
he chased the sun those early post-war years
in Cuernavaca, Taroudannt and Venice,
fleeing the gloom like Theseus whom he painted
for the Festival of Britain 1951.
Surreal humour flecked his visual palette:
pink pigs burst from the black earth like truffles,
as Greyhounds bussed him towards Omaha;
in Rome he marvelled at the riper vintage
of marbled genitals on the Campidoglio.

The interlocking of the human form
with what surrounds it, wrestling with wrestlers or
the empty landscape highly charged, bombarded
to fuse a new image, this remained his quest
as The Whitechapel crowned his fiftieth year
and other public recognition followed:
the honours list, the Royal College, Slade,
rich harvest for his art, his sun at zenith.
He only said the higher you go, the more
you leave the loved behind. A lost child's cry.

By the next decade he was mere survivor,
unloved. Unlived, the years were slipping away,
his friends dwindled and could not redeem him
from the sad mechanics of solitary drinking
and self-consuming sex that filled his diary,
into whose pages entered now, half welcome,
the recurring figure of Death, presaging cancer.
Poulenc's *Les Biches* still brought brief happiness,
music he knew from childhood like the taste
of his own tears; and if God had an image
to kneel before and worship, his would be
the face of the Egyptian boy king
Tutankamoun, gold mask with onyx eyes,
austere encouragement to go on trying.

'A sunny morning full of life' he wrote,
'the capsules have been taken with some whisky ...
.. ready for death though I fear it'. His final
words *'It wasn't a complete failure, I did some ..'* -
and here the printed text ends, marked [illegible].

But looking at the manuscript itself
under the glass case in that exhibition,
his dying hand was clear enough to me,
though faltering: *'I did some .. good work'.*

The Shillinged Birches

('There is only the fight to recover what has been lost')

I.

As the school-bus took the corner, wind lifted
the birch tree branches, shifting the light's angle.
Leaves shimmied in the sun, a heavenly jackpot
cascading a rush of shillings through green air.

That first lucid exposure, undeveloped
from the dark cells, emerged to no solution,
its figure only recurring as a remainder
down the long divisions of fifty years.

Others followed, each chance illumination
(say cutting a stick, or stepping over a stream)
held the singularity of the split second
in a sharp image whose quick I longed to reach.

Such flashes gone, their pungent drift would linger
like smoke over a conjuror's empty hat,
the watcher sensing his pockets begin to bulge
with the improbable doves. It was a trick

not turned, but visited on the open
mind at intervals, off guard, unawares:
a peep behind the curtain of unknowing,
a sudden flare from an alternate world.

II.

The gesture of the mandarin
secure within his painted hall
does not provide the palanquin
immunity against the fall.

Fixed points that marked the way
forget their bearings, and the crowds
that once tipped hats for time of day
hurl obscenities aloud.

Rites of passage, to define
present by past and future tense,
are now observed in their decline
to conjugate inconsequence.

Does the Church sound grave alarms
at forfeited authority?
O blessèd, blessèd be the psalms
that used to teach her harmony.

And why obey the Public Voice
enjoining all to trust or follow?
The march presents a Hobson's choice
to hear which drum sounds better hollow.

It is the inarticulate
whose counter *coup d'état* has come:
The fate of the graffiti State,
from whitewash too correctly done.

III.

Student, householder, forest-dweller, wandering
scholar, says *Yoga Over Fifty*: 'This picture shows
just how flexible someone in their eighties can be
after many years' practice' (She looks like a capital Q).

Not too late then to choose *asanas*, master the breath,
understand there is no dilemma to be unhorned,
accept like Roman poets that the heart which leaps
with the trout may leap at recognition promised.

The secret is to know the place for the first time
where one can escape from moving in the shadow
of another's assumptions. If in the public forum
there's still room for heightened speech,

for civility, its utterance may yet help make
some things not happen which are better avoided.
Monkeys chew fresh leaves in the dawn canopy :
below, we must bite on each coin newly minted.

Poem On the Underground

Up there words float like bubbles from his head,
catch fire above my fellow passenger,
lead us from inner darkness by a thread.

Sometimes their legend, read or left unread,
can ambush the unwitting traveller
when words float free, like bubbles from the head

of one who, dreaming, dives with sinking tread
to find lost treasure, and need only err
to waken airless, hanging by a thread.

Let us then light these tunnels of the dead,
and kiss the lips of the sweet messenger
whom the words float like bubbles from. Ahead

day beckons, and our *mappa mundi*'s spread
as tapestry on patient Ithaca
to pick and unpick daily by the thread.

No frippery, no fancy gingerbread –
to fine, to hone, to join, to disinter
words that go straight, like bubbles, to your head.
We are all saved from darkness by a thread.

Poem Found on the Underground

Stripped to the waist and shining
he joined at Piccadilly,
his border collie followed.
His white neighbour said 'Could you
move your dog, I'm allergic
to dogs', fingering the peak
of a baseball cap, on which
was emblazoned the single
Chinese character for 'sheep'.

Invitation

(Catullus: Carmen XIII)

Dear Fabullus,
           You will dine well at my place
this coming weekend, if our stars stay lucky,
provided you bring with you the wherewithal
of a good menu, bring also the bottles,
salt up your jokes, and don't forget the popsy.
If, old friend, you arrive equipped with all this,
you'll have a good meal. As for me (Catullus)
I find my wallet's filled only with cobwebs.
But in return I promise love's cocktails neat,
and, to show we're cool and still in the fast lane,
you may try the bouquet of *my* girl's perfume,
her own luxury 'Aura Amorosa'.
Once you've scented those pheromones, you will wish
Nature could make of you one huge proboscis!

Ripe Fruit

i.m. Colin Legum, died 2003 (Africa correspondent *The Observer* 1951-81)

Mangos unite us all,
you once said.
        I remember Mao
blessing and despatching them
to China's four corners
for Red Guards to dance and sing to.

To eat, circumcise their skin,
twist off one cloche,
suck flesh from bone
like a lollipop. Repeat.

Or, cleave length-wise twice
shaving the stone close,
score the scalped ellipses
as for noughts and crosses,
turned inside out
rubic-cube hedgehogs will
sit up and beg.

As I plunge in, the zest's dry
undertow on my tongue
recalls the ebb
and flow of your persistent cast
over waters where
rainbow colours were already hinting at
that patient revolution,
your final greatest catch.

May Lane, Birmingham

(After *Gardeners' World*)

His coriander shooting green tongues,
over his rake Mohammed Ali says
people who do allotments aren't made.

Bean-sticks, bird scarers, plastic bottles
stake out these patchwork acres where
you follow string straight down the rows

or skip a sort of ballerina hop-scotch
from one to another, not surprised to see
rumps rear up like errant cantaloups.

Jahangir Singh navigates with care
to nurse his crop of marrows and courgettes
as one who ferries souls to their salvation.

Whipping thoroughbred race-horse manure
to curds of liquid amber guarantees
Thomas's dahlias beat all the odds.

While Arthur sticks to planting Kestrel spuds,
for gooseberry juice calypso-style Cynthia
spikes her mix with Guinness on the spot.

Ask Teresinha how she grows colours,
fermenting leaves to bleed wode on cloth
dipped to deepen bluer under daylight –

they are like photographs developing:
Friends discovered clutching their first fruits –
a perfect set, growing together, laughing.

Elizabeth's Version

I could wish, brother, more poetry in him,
less theatre. To scotch Valentines on a whim,
how childish. He thinks I pray at St Olave's
just for the dancing master? Look how I slave
all the year round – I doubt that enters into
his crotchety short-hand. And it's no sin to
lift French minuet above *cazzo dritto*.
I love him, but he risks my love's memento
engrossed with hot tongs where they cut out his stone.
'Prick-louse' must change his tune, or trill to atone!

Stomachful? Yes, I put it all down to fear
the ancient name might founder without an heir.
His bobbin threadless, how could I close the stitch?
So, plagued by his own pest, fired by an itch
to fumble every skirt, he would gad about
like some periwigged Polcinello, played out,
mocked from the quarterdeck. Then pity whispered
'The heart may soon grow sick when hope is deferred:
bolder jointure is easy for your beauty
to conceive – call it a catholic duty.'

His fishmonger uncle had already asked
to sire my child for gold (what cod!). But the task
was now to catch seed blown from farther afield,
to spring home-grown. With a birth, I knew he'd yield
and his lion be caged. To Brampton by coach
I fell in with a King's Guard man, whose approach
brought back at once the Lambeth gypsy's riddle
'Fortune's messenger will not ride side-saddle'.
We broke the day's passage at The Reindeer Inn.
By candle, many would have been taken in.

A small bird fluttered, and I rejoiced to hide
belly in billowing morning gown. Outside,
Dutch ships sailed up the Thames, and the press of war
kept him as distant as the evening star.
I never told him. But when I lost the child,
feigning simply my months had returned, he smiled
as if some gibbous thought half-formed in his mind,
then turned back to prospects for *The Golden Hand*
and Navy business. As I have since turned back
to painting Our Saviour, and my sun is black.

*(Elizabeth de St Michel, wife to Samuel Pepys, died on 10 November 1669
at the age of 29, and was buried in St Olave's Church, Hart Street)*

Moving with THE TIMES

(13 April 2003)

The clue for 20 across (7) reads
'How the past differs from the present'.
Ask Arthur Bryant & Malcolm Muggeridge,
whose *Course on Democracy* sounds intense.
Run a finger down the agony column:
note calls for unwanted artificial teeth;
£12 for *Thucydides* in mint condition;
for rheumatism, colonic irrigation.

I see a lady wishes to dispose,
privately, of her Rolls-Royce Phantom,
and that her chauffeur's 'open for engagement'
(a garage with telephone is also free).
Perhaps she'll use the proceeds to acquire
the ARP garden trench shelter –
a dozen dwarf Michaelmas daisies make
immense cushions, lilac, mauve or blue.

Next page the Lord Chancellor, giving judgment,
says the question is what does the word 'proportion'
    mean.
Revue's non-stop at the Windmill Piccadilly;
'*Wild Oats*' is playing at The Prince's.
Frost being less severe in the Vale of Evesham,
the asparagus crop has escaped damage.
In Saskatchewan drought-stricken farmers
send messages along their wire fences.

Obituaries mark the death of Schaliapin.
General Franco's troops have resumed
their advance to the sea. Allied experts
discuss the future size of battleships.
One hundred and forty-seven successive loops
have set a new record for a glider.
The RAF has vacancies for pilots.
Time-bomb explosion kills two in Haifa.

The ayes and noes have tied in the Commons:
The Member for Hexham said the motion only
added to Arab fears in Palestine –
the Speaker voted for the Bill giving
every migrant there the rights of citizen.
The Stock Market remains mostly steady.
I notice pure silk hailspot foulard's used
for a charming new frock from Debenhams.

Mothers are warned to keep babies from air
raid demonstrations. The pelts of Russian
dyed ermine make perfectly fitting boleros.
'Conquer your *nerves*! Write for the free book!'
My birthday puzzle make no fitting sense
for those who'd understand the human state:
the clues today differ only I-N T-E-N-S-E
from 13 April 1938.

Dénouement

It is not the regular
cut of her diamond nor her collar

of pearls but the blue
of her jugular vein I value

above lapis lazuli or sapphire stone.
My work is done.

While I wait for them to arrive
I shall not grieve

for that would change the story
in my book. I shall write more

now I have time. The trouble with balance
is, you can lose it only once.

IV. Cycle of Cathay

Nocturne

(After The Lute Song of Po Chü-I, ad 815)

One night I rode down to the Hsünyang river
to see a friend off. Maple leaf and bulrush
nodded an autumn *envoi*, and his boat lay
ready for him to launch as I dismounted.

We drank to each other, yet without music
the wine-cups only left us sadder to part;
the moon's face blurred in the watery vastness . . .
Then from nowhere along the river sounded

a pi-pa lute! Forgetting all departure
we called towards it, tracked its source in the dark,
edged the boat closer for an invitation –
the music broke off, silence was the solo.

'Bring on the wine! Light lamps! Set out the table!'
To our halloos and cheers she at last emerged,
holding the lute as if to cover her face,
fine-tuned the pegs, and strummed a flourish of notes.

Before melody we recognised passion,
as if some force breathed into and possessed her
when she played and sang her darkly coloured songs,
her open encyclopaedia of love.

She leaned intently to pick out from the strings
delicate riffs undressing our defences –
'Rainbow Petticoat', 'Green Waist', cascades of pearls
pouring on jade salvers, the oriole's call.

Each time with sobbing chords, mouth full of pebbles,
the voice welled up in her throat like a fountain
till its silver flask shattered, till emotion
spilled out its cavalry charge straight to the heart.

Resting her lute, she composed herself again:
'I come from the capital, my home Hsiamo.
At thirteen a virtuoso of the art,
I outplayed my peers at the conservatoire.

The women all envied my looks. The young men
from Wuling plied me with presents – one song, and
bolts of scarlet silk would rain down at my door.
Beating time, they'd knock gold and silver to bits!

Then my brother went to war, and my aunt died.
The sky changed colour; it was cold and lonely.
I put on years; became wife to a merchant,
who chased profit, made light of separation.

Last month he travelled to Fuliang to buy tea,
leaving me at the river mouth, boat empty.
One dead of night I was dreaming of my youth:
I awoke to find my rouged face streaked with tears.'

Her words set off such echoes that I answered
'We are both like lost souls in the wilderness,
thrown together by fate, no need to explain.
Last year I too had to leave the capital –

exiled, I live on my sick-bed at Hsünyang,
a down-at-heel sort of place, with no music.
All year round no strings or pipes, just low-lying
swamps of yellow madder and bitter bamboo.

Morning to dusk what do I hear? The nightjar
mourning its hours out and the monkey howling.
Not the flowers of spring nor autumn moonshine
save me from drinking into lonely collapse.

I'm bored by hill yodels and village ditties.
Tonight your songs were a sublime recital
suddenly rinsing my ears. Play me some more,
let me add my own verses to your cycle.'

Overcome she faltered ... turned back to her lute,
but played instead a most haunting threnody
which left all of us speechless – none more than this
neighbourhood clerk, crying into my blue robe.

Translations from Mao

Changsha

Alone in the autumn cold I stand,
where the Hsiang River heads North
past the tip of Orange Island.
The mountains are all turning red,
as fall dyes the forest steeps.
The green water's clear as glass,
barges crowding downstream.
Through the high air eagles beat,
fish hang below in shallows.
All kind vie for freedom, this frosty day.
Unnerved by such vastness,
I ask the great globe
who rules life's ups and downs?

I used to bring here many friends,
heady times I remember well.
Young schoolmates
in our exuberant prime,
the student spirit fired us
to put muscle into words.
Pointing the finger at all China,
how we brandished our philippics.
Those lords in their great mansions: pure shit!

Do you remember
going down to swim, slapping the water,
how our waves rocked the light sampans?

(1925. Mao Tse-tung recalls his early years in native Hunan)

Chung Yang Festival

It is man who grows old, the world is almost ageless.
Year on year, the Double Ninth.
Today it's come round again,
the battlefield is heavy with the scent of yellow blossom.
On time with the season, an autumn wind stiffens.
The light is not like spring's,
it has outshone the light of spring,
from river to horizon the vast landscape is ablaze with
    frost.

(1929. Ninth day of the ninth moon, when ancestors' graves are visited. After early victories in Fukien)

The Long March

Our Red Army shrank from
no long march hardships.
We took them in our stride,
mountains and waters.

The Five Ranges rippled
patterns of small waves,
Wumeng's summits spilled like
children's mud puddings.

Cliff clouds at Gold Sand gave
warmth to the river:
but on Tatu's chain bridge
our hands stuck frozen.

Happy at last to see
far snows of Minshan,
once our columns had crossed
we burst out laughing!

(1935. Completion of Mao's year-long 6000 mile march to Yenan)

Snow

Here is the Northern landscape
icebound into the distance.
A huge expanse of swirling snow.
On both sides of the Great Wall
I see only vast steppes.
Upstream and down, the Yellow River
suddenly looks almost sluggish.
The mountains dance their silver snake,
like shining elephants the highlands roll
clambering to reach the Lord of Heaven.
Let the sun shine, and
in her white dress laced with red
nature will ravish us –
her rivers and mountains are so beautiful,
she has brought legions of heroes to their knees.

Alas, the first emperors of Chin and Han
had no skill to turn a phrase.
The founding fathers of Tang and Sung
could barely whistle downwind.
Even great Genghis Khan's art
reached only to drawing his bow at the eagle.
All have gone into the past.
For men of stature, free spirits,
the new age dawns today.

(1936. Probably written at Yenan)

Capture of Nanking

On Bell Peak the storm breaks
steel-blue and yellow.
Over the Yangtze pass
one million warriors.

Nanking, you crouched tiger,
you dragon mountain,
your world stands on its head.
We are big-hearted –

but 'sparing the spent foe'
is not our maxim:
Three Kingdoms warns against
praise bought with mercy.

They say 'if God could feel,
he too would grow old',
– watch us turn his Vast to
fields of mulberry!

(1949. Mao finally ousts Chiang Kai-shek from his Southern capital)

Answering Mr Liu Ya-tzu

I still recall how we
drank tea in Canton:
thought up rhymes at Chungking,
as leaves turned yellow.

After thirty-one years
back in old Peking,
petals fall while I read
your limpid verses.

Beware, a heart can break
from too much grumbling.
Clear eye and far sight bring
the world perspective.

You find 'the capital's
lake is too shallow'?
More fish to watch than in
your Southern river!

(1949. Installed after final victory in Peking, Mao counsels a poet friend against returning to the quiet life)

Swimming

First I gulped water at Changsha,
now at Wuchang, swallowing fish,
I am swimming across the endless River Yangtze.
This kingdom's sky stretches out of sight.
No matter how wind blows and waves buffet,
it's better than kicking my heels on the porch.
Today I count plenty of time remaining:
what did Confucius say on the bank of his stream?
'Dying must be like this passing flow'.

Squall shakes the mastheads,
Tortoise and Snake Hills lie quiet.

Up floats another brainwave! –
A bridge with flying arches
shall span nature's moat and lay a highway South to
     North;
then we'll build a stone dam against the river from the
     West
to cut the flow and deal with Wushan's rainclouds.
The high gorges shall raise a calm lake.

If the Mountain Goddess is not indisposed,
she'll have to marvel at her changed world.

(1956. At 63 Mao swims the Yangtze from Wuchang to Hankow)

For Li Shu-yi

I lost my tough poplar and you your willow.
Our Poppy and Will soared to the ninth heaven.
They asked the Moon's Prisoner to tell them all:
Wu Kang held out to them cassia-flower wine.
The Lonely Chang O spread voluminous sleeves,
for two faithful souls she danced across the sky.
Then, from the world below, news of Tiger's defeat –
tears came flooding down: it was raining buckets.

(1957. Mao recalls to a woman friend their respective spouses' earlier war-deaths,
punning the names)

Goodbye to the God of Plagues

I.

They're out of place, all these
blue hills, green waters,
while a tiny blood-fluke
trumps our best doctors.

Whole villages in weeds,
men's bowels pouring,
houses left empty to
gibbering spectres.

Each day the Earth spins me
round on its axle,
sweeping the skies I scan
untold galaxies.

From the stars Herd Boy asks:
what of the Plague God?
Sad or happy, we must
counter his death-wave.

II.

A spring breeze lifts the wands
of crowding willows.
God's country's millions match
golden age virtue.

Red blossoms, and becomes
a sea of pennants,
those same blue hills we see
turn into bridges.

From China's Five Peaks to
her great Three Rivers,
the glint and clangour
of pick and mattock!

Beg your pardon, Lord Plague,
would you be leaving?
we'll mark your going with
paper boats, candles.

(1958. Filling infected ponds and ditches helps eliminate bilharzia)

Back to Shaoshan

Losing a dream is like
a small bereavement:
thirty-two years since I
left these home acres.

Later the red flag urged
serfs to their halberds,
for a black hand still held
the whip of tyrants.

Our will was resolute
sacrifice easy.
We challenged sun and moon
to a new heaven.

Look now, rice and bean fields,
a sea of harvest,
the heroes coming home,
dusk falling like smoke.

(1959. Mao returns to his native village from which he had fled in 1927)

Winter Clouds

Snow swirls from winter clouds
like flocks of cotton,
settles as countless blooms
which fade and vanish.

High above, icy streams
plunge tumbling,tumbling:
here on low ground, the air
seems almost balmy.

It takes heroes to quell
tiger and leopard:
a brave man does not fear
the mountain grizzly.

A flowering plum-tree
welcomes the snow-flakes.
Dung-flies freezing to death
perish unnoticed.

*(1962. Composed on Mao's 69th birthday, with references
to the Sino-Soviet Dispute)*

Peking Rap

I.

The Queen's Messenger was late. A mob at the gate
had swelled all morning. Another warning
never got through: friends knew
something was afoot – lads on foot
with full jerry-cans spelled plans.
Telephone cut, couldn't get out –
sentries: 'Don't, or China won't
be responsible'. Quite impossible
not to laugh, so we didn't half-
roar at the Peter Sellers movie.
Off-screen, suddenly, it was moving:

II.

Our man's just bid three-no-trumps
when the night roars back, and we catch a glimpse
of a Verey flare as a surge of bodies
over the wall floods up towards us,
'THEY'RE COMING IN!'
followed by the din
of pole-axed doors, burst windows:
shock---, blitz--- , bangs--- , blows!
The twenty-three of us trapped alone
fall back fast to the strong-room zone,
while ten thousand light the flame
for their once-in-a-lifetime bonfire game,
and the Lion & the Unicorn's sole defence
pleads *honi soit qui mal y pense.*
Sparks leap up, smoke gets thicker,
breath in this small room comes quicker;
stuff gushes through the window bars,
Red Guards shouting 'sha! sha!'
(better not translate for the ladies).
Fire now rages, hot as Hades,
bricks cave in as a pile drives through,
(might get stuck if the door jams to).

Some of us wonder: is this moment
how we'll know our final moment?
Out we stagger to a screaming mass
of our fellow-creatures having a gas
as they gouge and punch and twist and tear,
and somebody's pulling out my wife's hair,
and someone else rips off her pants,
lewd prying fingers leave their prints,
my teeth bite deeper into his arm,
down we go to the stinging swarm.
Our man floats off with a blood-drenched face.
While we're locked in hate's embrace,
arc lights glare and a camera whirrs
to shoot us live, and the *cri de guerre*'s
'Tell your crimes and bow your head
you English dogs, or you'll be dead!'

III.
One of us did die not long after,
another lay motionless for weeks,
one went mad for a year. Laughter
was not why it hurt to speak.

Now, as I hear the spool unwind
my distant, dated, plummy voice,
this brush with danger sounds small beer
compared with those who'd had no choice:

the millions who the Great Leap Forward
starved to death for a Party phrase;
the millions who'd been 'rectified'
or suicide cut short whose days;

a nation's children who we watched
forfeit their school years and their youth,
for whom denouncing parents was
the recommended way to truth.

I bow to China and her beauty,
and hold no grudge, just this conclusion:
let Mao be judged by history,
and f___ all bloody revolution!

*(On 22 August 1967, a Red Guard mob burned down the British Diplomatic
Mission in Peking and beat up its occupants who were prevented from leaving
China for the next 18 months)*

Snuff Bottles

They take me back to old Peking, dusty
hu-t'ungs in the South city, where we biked
through browncoal reek, past toffee-apple stalls
seeking the thin-paned door hidden by Mao
posters, behind whose promises eclipsed
a pensioner arranged his dying stars.

Hair-crystal, amethyst, beeswax amber,
malachite, jasper, agate, ink-stone, jet,
aquamarine, fossilised mammoth tooth,
they lay carved where he'd placed them in his drawer,
as one by one owners cashed at market
family heirlooms they dared not bequeath.

Each with stopper drawing ivory spoon,
no taller than a thumb, like trim vessels
they compassed little worlds within their world,
cargoes en route since Emperor Ch'ien Lung,
that held the ballast for their snuffy smells
enclosed in cockleshells whose form was art.

I loved the glass ampul, inside-painted
by Lo-yüan's keyhole brush, and how his birds
moved in the pine-trees, boys' kites came alive;
loved the shaped stone, its own poem engraved
'As if this jade is covered with white clouds
and green peaks pierce them here and there above.'

Collector's itch now mostly seems escape –
from the embassy's burning, from Red Guards'
murdered victims lying in the gutter,
the mindless ransack. Did it stand for hope
that care for small things might move us towards
a better state? So much, then, the better.

Back in London we sold our collection
to furnish our first home, and since that month
burglars cleaned us out, it was just as well.
The clue to this unlooked for repossession:
'Chinese Snuff Bottles' fell off the bookshelf.
In the end I never found a hornbill.

Mathews' Chinese Dictionary

I sift through: a peach leaf skeleton
    with pressed butterfly comes sailing out
as if to flag the resurrection
    of sleeping souls, characters that shout

to be found again after decades
    of silence, lest we forget about
what's passed (wasn't it Whitman who said

'Who touches this book, touches a man'?)
    From China Inland Mission, Shanghai
1931, Mathews began
    to transmit *en clair*, to all who'd try

'the task of learning this great language'.
    The leaf veins are etched fields, seen from high
in space, on some returning voyage.

To re-enter his pages is to
    come upon a familiar house, where
if one has the key one can go through
    windows to the wider view: look, there –

the covers open on a country
    whose Great Wall declares a world's wonder
to the moon, each piece of masonry

a stone poem, in a word: graphic
    Long March that reaches from Han to Mao
through centuries no alphabetic
    code could rival (who knows Beowulf now,

untutored?) I say this book's a sky
    seeded with endless meteor showers
which shoot, blossom in the reader's eye.

The script's no movie-show written in
        pictures for imagists. No, it's the
chemistry excites the retina,
        the cut gems of meaning, the glitter

of their collisions and reactions,
        their resistance to time or grammar.
From 'Three Kingdoms' to Red Guard factions,

a butterfly can still cause chaos
        with its entry: 'rainbow, sphenoid bone,
shops in an arcade, hinge, fleur-de-lys,'
        or pun for 'old man' whose days have flown –

as this one soared in final flight,
        who left a variousness that shone
like a comet streaming hairs of light.